Walter Foster®

The Incredible Kids' Craft-IT Series

Concoct IT

Written and crafted by Pam Thomson

Illustrated by Jeff Shelly

Concoct It Contents

Getting Started

When you mix together a recipe of fun, imagination, and cool ideas, you'll easily blast away boredom! Concoct It is chock-full of crazy concoctions—from dinosaur eggs to puffy-paint games—made with common kitchen and craft supplies. In no time at all, you'll have a whole slew of "uniquely you" crafts to enjoy—and to show off to family and friends!

Check the "Get It" list with a grownup before you start your concoctions so you can get some help gathering up your materials. (Sometimes you might need an adult's help with a project, just to be safe.) In addition to your supplies and your grownup, find some old rags or newspaper to cover your workspace—your parents will appreciate it if you keep things clean!

Most of the supplies in Concoct It (such as flour or salt) come straight from your cupboards, but art and craft supply stores have great selections of other materials you might need. Check out the bead section for fun decorative pieces, and try the soap or candle-making section for materials like soap molds and scented oil. And if a Concoct It activity calls for a pattern, look to the back of the book, where you'll find a special tear-out section of all the patterns you'll need. If you want to make a pattern bigger or smaller to customize your project, ask an adult to help you duplicate it on a photocopier.

Once you get started, you'll find that the projects shown in this book are just the beginning of your concocting adventures. Feel free to substitute materials or make changes that suit your personal style. Don't hold back—be as creative and imaginative as you can, and make your projects as original as you are!

Look for this symbol to let you know when a grownup's help is needed.

⚠ Watch It!
Look for this symbol to let you know when special care or precautions are needed.

Splashy Salts and Flavorful Gloss

When you follow these super-easy recipes, you'll be whipping up a simply beautiful batch of fun and relaxation!

Small jars are perfect containers for fun and fruity lip gloss concoctions. Decorate them with flowers, puffy paint, ribbon roses, or even glitter and jewels to make your lip gloss really shine!

For a great gift, make a single-bath-sized sachet using a small fabric bag tied with ribbon.

Get It!

1 cup (250 ml) coarse rock salt
Food coloring
Scented oil
4 test tubes
4 cork stoppers (for the test tubes)
Mixing spoon
Small mixing bowl
Funnel
Ribbon roses
Ribbon
White craft glue
Pen
Small round, self-stick labels or gift tags

Scented Bath Crystals

1 In a bowl, use a spoon to mix the salt together with 3–4 drops of food coloring, or as much as you need to get the color you want. Add 5 drops of scented oil and mix well.

2 Using the funnel, pour the salts into the test tubes and insert the corks. Tie some ribbon around the top of the test tube, and glue the knot to the glass. Glue a ribbon rose on top of the knot.

TWO TABLESPOONS PER BATH

3 Write, "Two tablespoons per bath" ("30 ml per bath") on a round label or gift tag, and stick or glue it to the top of the cork stopper.

⚠️ **Watch It!**

The melted oil will be hot!
Ask a grownup to help you pour it.

Get it!

2 ounces (60 grams)
    powdered drink mix
2 tablespoons (30 ml) solid
    vegetable shortening
Pill box or small container with lid
Microwave-safe pitcher
Assorted ribbons and ribbon roses
White craft glue
Mixing spoon

Flavored Lip Gloss

1 Stir the drink mix and the shortening together, and microwave the mixture on high until it is completely melted (30–60 seconds).

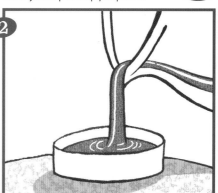

2 Pour the mixture into the container, and let it cool until it's solid again. Decorate the lid by using glue to attach ribbon and roses.

"Candy" Soap

Make glycerin soaps that look good enough to eat! These petal-perfect gifts are great for washing—but not for snacking!

You can make store-bought soap pretty too! Cover the smooth side with water-based glue sealer. When dry, stencil designs using acrylic craft paint.

You can also pour soap into a shallow pan to cut out cool shapes with cookie cutters!

Get It!

2-pound (1 kg) brick of glycerin soap
Small soap molds or candy molds
Food coloring
1-pint (500 ml) microwave-safe
    measuring cup
Tiny silk flower heads
    (plastic backing removed)
Large silk flower
    (plastic backing removed)
Paper candy cups
Decorative box
Ribbon
Toothpick
Kitchen knife
Mixing spoon
White craft glue
Scented oil or soap fragrance (optional)

1 Have a grownup help you cut five 1" (2.5 cm) cubes from the glycerin brick and place them in the measuring cup. Microwave on high for 40 seconds. Continue to heat for 10 seconds at a time until the soap is completely melted.

2 To make colored shapes, stir the food coloring into the melted soap before pouring the soap into the molds. If you want to make your soaps scented, you can add 2–4 drops of scented oil or soap fragrance now.

3 Fill the molds halfway with melted soap. Place the flower heads face down in the poured soap, and use a toothpick to push the heads half-way down into the soap. Pour in more melted soap to fill the mold. Let cool for 20–30 minutes.

4 Apply gentle pressure to the front of the mold to release the soap shapes. Place each of the finished shapes into a candy cup, and arrange the soaps however you like in the bottom of your decorative box.

5 Lay the ribbon across the box lid. Fold both ends under the box lip, and secure it with glue. Trim off any excess, and then glue the flower on top.

⚠ **Watch It!**
• Melted soap will be very hot!
  Ask a grownup to help you pour.
• No matter how yummy these soaps look,
  they should never be eaten!

Spacey Scratchboard Art

Peer deep into the darkness and what do you see? Vibrant pictures and mesmerizing designs!

When you scratch through the ink layers, your true colors will come shining through, and your artistic genius will really stand out!

Get It!

All-media illustration board
(or substitute white cardboard
or poster board)
Black India ink or black crayon
Colored wax crayons
Medium paintbrush
Metal nail file

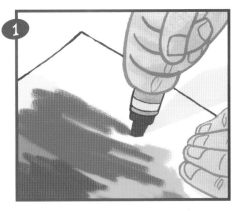

1

Use different colors of crayons to cover the entire illustration board. Use heavy pressure to make sure each area is completely covered. (Bright or fluorescent colors will show up especially well.) Overlap the colors where they meet to cover the entire surface of the board.

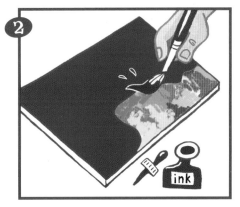

2

Cover your work surface with newspaper to protect it from spills. Then brush one coat of India ink over the whole board (or cover all the colored patches with black crayons). Let it dry, and apply a second coat of India ink. Coat four to five times or until the crayon does not show through the ink.

3

Use the end of the file to "draw" a design by scratching through the layers of India ink or black crayon, exposing the colors underneath.

⚠ Watch It!
India ink is permanent and can stain your clothes and carpets. Be careful!

Moon Rocks and Dinosaur Eggs

Blast off to the moon or back to the past when you create your own moon rocks or dino eggs—with a surprise inside!

Glow-in-the-dark moon rocks can hide high-bouncing balls—or any other fun-n-funky party favors!

Decorate your dinosaur eggs with polka dots, stripes, and other prehistoric patterns, and conceal the dinosaurs inside!

Get It!

1 cup (250 ml) flour
1 cup (250 ml) used coffee grounds
½ cup (125 ml) salt
¼ cup (60 ml) sand
¾ cup (175 ml) water
Large mixing bowl
Mixing spoon
Glow-in-the-dark paint
Dry tempera paint, any color
Acrylic paints
Party favors
Small or medium paintbrush

1

Mix the first four ingredients together in the mixing bowl. Add 2 tablespoons (30 ml) of dry tempera paint and mix well. Add the water slowly, stirring and then kneading with your fingers until the mixture feels like smooth bread dough.

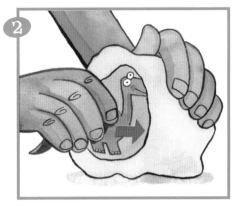

2

Break off a piece of dough big enough to completely cover your party favor. Make a hole in the dough, and then push in the favor. Seal the hole completely with dough. Air-dry for 3–5 days or until hard.

3

Paint the dry moon rocks with three coats of glow-in-the-dark paint, letting them dry between coats. Sit the rocks out in the sunlight for 8 hours.

Imagine It!
For more sparkle in your moon rocks, add glitter to the dry ingredients.

4

Paint the dinosaur eggs with acrylic paints, using wild patterns and bright colors. Let each coat of paint dry before adding the next color.

5

Smash the rocks or eggs on the ground to release the surprise inside!

Bedazzling No-Bake Jewelry

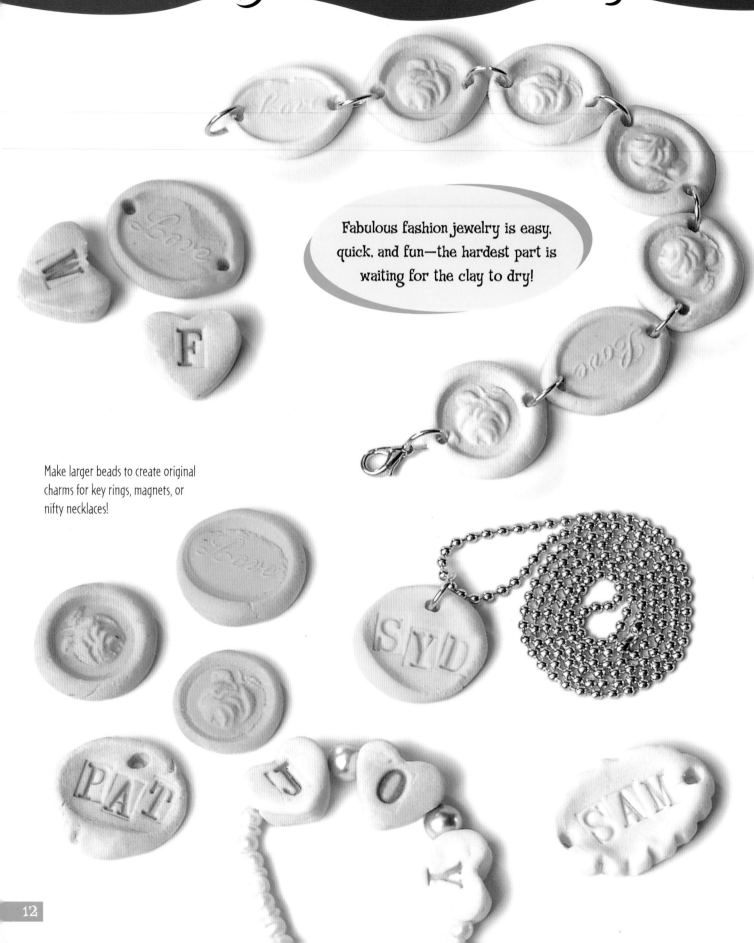

Fabulous fashion jewelry is easy, quick, and fun—the hardest part is waiting for the clay to dry!

Make larger beads to create original charms for key rings, magnets, or nifty necklaces!

Get It!

2-quart (2 L) saucepan
2 cups (500 ml) baking soda
1 cup (250 ml) cornstarch
1¼ cups (310 ml) cold water
Aluminum foil
Cookie sheet
Dish towel
Bamboo skewer
    or knitting needle
Food coloring
Embossing items (like shells, rubber
    stamps, or wax sealing stamps)
Jewelry jump rings and clasps
Acrylic paint
Elastic thread
Small or medium paintbrush
Small pliers
Oven mitt or potholder
Rubber gloves

Mix the soda and cornstarch together in the saucepan. Then add the water. Over medium heat, stir constantly for 10–15 minutes, until the mix has a pastelike texture. Pour the clay onto a piece of foil, and cover it with a damp dish towel until cool.

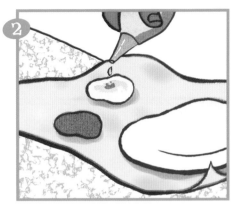

Take a small amount of the clay and add drops of food coloring, one at a time. Wearing rubber gloves, knead the clay after each drop until the color is absorbed. Repeat until you achieve your desired color.

Roll the colored clay into ½" (1.5 cm) balls, and emboss a design on top by pressing the ball firmly with a stamp or seal.

Make two holes on opposite sides of the seals with the bamboo skewer. Place the finished beads on a cookie sheet to air dry for 2–3 days.

After the beads are dry, you can paint them if you choose. Next attach the jewelry jump rings to each hole, string the beads together, and add the clasp.

Imagine It!

• Clay recipe (step 1) can be stored in the refrigerator in a sealed container for up to 2 weeks.
• Use an emery board to file off the rough edges of the dried clay.

⚠ Watch It!

• Ask a grownup to help with heating and baking.
• Food coloring can stain, so be sure to protect your work area and your clothing.

Colorful Clay Creations

How about some instant satisfaction? These bake-and-wear creations are sure to impress your friends!

Whether you make a mirror for your locker or an ornament for a tree, these colorful and crafty concoctions are always a bright idea!

Rocky

Get It!

1 1/4 cups (310 ml) flour
1 1/4 cups (310 ml) salt
1 tablespoon (15 ml) cooking oil
5/8 cup (150 ml) water
Cookie sheet
Shortening (to grease cookie sheet)
Rolling pin
Cookie cutters
Medium mixing bowl
Mixing spoon
Bamboo skewer or
    knitting needle
Craft paint
Small or medium paintbrush
Decorative items
    (such as buttons, beads, jewels, mirrors)
Ribbon or plastic lacing
White craft glue
Magnets or jewelry findings (like clasps, jump
    rings, earrings studs, or button covers)
Oven mitt or potholder

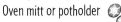

1

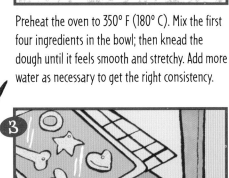

Preheat the oven to 350° F (180° C). Mix the first four ingredients in the bowl; then knead the dough until it feels smooth and stretchy. Add more water as necessary to get the right consistency.

2

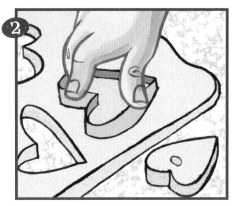

Roll out the dough to about 1/4" (6 mm) thickness. Then cut out shapes with a cookie cutter. Use a bamboo skewer to poke holes in the pieces where you plan to hang or thread them.

3

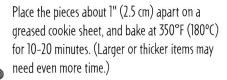

Place the pieces about 1" (2.5 cm) apart on a greased cookie sheet, and bake at 350°F (180°C) for 10–20 minutes. (Larger or thicker items may need even more time.)

4

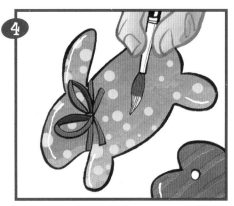

When the pieces are dry, paint them, let them dry, and then add decorative items of your choice. Glue on magnets or add jewelry findings to finish your colorful creations.

Imagine It!
Use an emery board to file off any rough edges on the dried clay.

⚠ Watch It!
Ask a grownup to help you with baking.

Pop-ular Bubble Boxes

Here's a craft you can really get wrapped up in—pretty papers that are bubbling over with fun!

Mix paint and dish soap to make these bubble-designed boxes—perfect for holding all your little treasures!

Get It!

8-1/2" x 11" (21 x 29.5 cm) sheets of colored
    paper (such as bond paper or craft paper)
2 teaspoons (10 ml) clear liquid detergent
1/4 cup (60 ml) liquid tempera paint
Medium or large paintbrush
Water
Drinking straw
Small mixing bowl
Mixing spoon

Bubble Paper

1 With a paintbrush, mix the detergent and the tempera paint together in the bowl. Add about 3 tablespoons (45 ml) of water. (The more water you use, the weaker the color will be.)

2 Put the straw into the mixture, and then blow through it to make bubbles in the bowl. The bubbles should rise above the lip of the bowl. (But don't let them spill over!)

3 Hold the paper over the bowl, and gently dab the paper on the bubbles, letting the bubbles pop on the paper.

4 Continue blowing and dabbing until the paper is completely covered with the bursted bubble design. Let the paper dry completely.

⚠ Watch It!

When making the bubbles, always be careful to blow *out* through the straw. Tempera paint is nontoxic, so although it won't really hurt you if you happen to suck some in your mouth, it isn't any fun!

Get It!

Flower box pattern (page 33)
8-$\frac{1}{2}$" x 11" (21 x 29.5 cm) sheet of
  finished bubble paper
Ribbon
Ruler
Pencil
Scissors
Hole punch
White glue

Flower Box

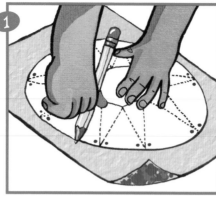

1 Trace the pattern onto the back of your paper. Be sure to copy all the dotted fold lines and hole markings. Cut out the tracing.

2 Following the pattern you traced, fold the paper inward along all the dotted fold lines as shown. Then press over the creases with your thumbnail.

3 Punch out the holes as marked on your pattern, and then lace your ribbon through the holes so the ribbon begins and ends on the outside of the box. Put your gift inside, cinch the bag shut, and tie a bow!

Imagine It!

If you want to reinforce the bottom of the box, trace the octagon bottom onto cardboard. Then cut out the cardboard bottom, and paste it inside the paper box with white glue.

Get It!

Seashell box pattern (page 35)
8 1/2" x 11" (21 x 29.5 cm) sheet of
    finished bubble paper
Pencil
Scissors
Hole punch
Fabric fastener circles, like Velcro™
White glue
Ribbon or fabric trim
Shell

Seashell Box

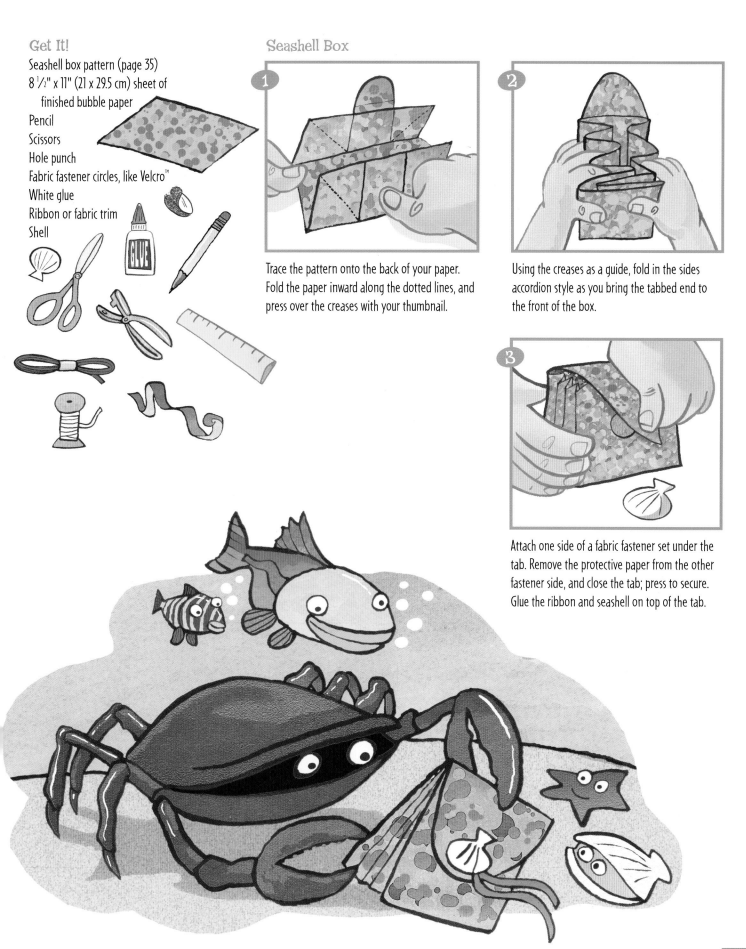

1 Trace the pattern onto the back of your paper. Fold the paper inward along the dotted lines, and press over the creases with your thumbnail.

2 Using the creases as a guide, fold in the sides accordion style as you bring the tabbed end to the front of the box.

3 Attach one side of a fabric fastener set under the tab. Remove the protective paper from the other fastener side, and close the tab; press to secure. Glue the ribbon and seashell on top of the tab.

Yellow mustard creates
super-cool swirly patterns
on white fabric—
just don't try this craft
if you're hungry!

You can turn "playing with your food" into an art form when you paint with yellow mustard!

Get It!

17" (42.5 cm) square of cotton fabric
(enough to make two scarves)
1 yard (1 meter) white cording
Squeeze bottle of yellow mustard
2 decorative beads
1 cup (250 ml) vinegar
1/4" (6 mm) iron-on fusible hemming
tape or fabric glue
Colored rhinestones
Scissors
Ruler
Iron (for fusible tape only)

1 Fold the cloth in half diagonally, and cut it into two equal triangles. Squeeze the mustard bottle to apply a free-form pattern to the cloth. Let the mustard sit for 1 hour, and then wash it off with cool water.

2 Set the color and design by soaking the cloth in a sink filled with tap water mixed with 1 cup (250 ml) of vinegar. Let the cloth soak in the mixture for about 15 minutes. Then hang the bandanna somewhere inside to dry.

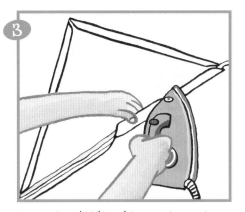

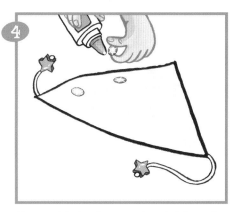

3 Fuse or glue a 1/4" (6 mm) hem on the two short sides of the triangle. Then lay the cording inside a 1/2" (1.5 cm) hem fold on the longer side. Fuse or glue the edge only, keeping the cord free.

4 Slip one of the beads onto each end of the cording, and knot the bottom of both sides of the cording to prevent the beads from sliding off. Glue on rhinestones to decorate the fabric, and allow it to dry.

Imagine It!
- Use a large white handkerchief instead of buying cloth. It will already have two sides hemmed when cut into two triangles.
- If you plan to wash the scarf, reinforce the hem by hand or machine stitching.

⚠ Watch It!
Keep a grownup handy for the ironing.

Playful Puffy-Paint Games

Around the pool, at the beach, or in the bathtub, these colorful game pieces are great for playtime—anytime!

Need more ideas? Make your mark with a set of tic-tac-toe pieces created with craft foam and glitter glue!

Get It! (Puffy Paint)

¼ cup (60 ml) white craft glue
Powdered tempera paint
¼ teaspoon (1 ml) cornstarch
Mixing spoon
1-pint (500 ml) measuring
   pitcher with spout
2-4 ounce (60-120 g) empty
   squeeze bottle with cap

Puffy Paint

1. In the pitcher, mix the glue and cornstarch together well. To start, add about a teaspoon (5 ml) of powdered tempera; then add more until it's the color you want.
2. Pour the paint into the squeeze bottle, and screw on the cap.

Get It! (Glitter Glue)

¼ cup (60 ml) white glue
Assorted glitter
   (fine grade works best)
Mixing spoon
1-pint (500 ml) measuring
   pitcher with spout
2-4 ounce (60-120 g) empty
   squeeze bottle with cap

Glitter Glue

1. In the pitcher, mix about ⅛ cup (30 ml) of glitter with about ¼ cup (60 ml) of glue.
2. Pour the glue into the squeeze bottle, and screw on the cap.

Tip: If your glitter is coarser than fine grade, use more glue and wider mouthed squeeze bottles.

Get It! (Poolside Dominoes)

Domino dot pattern (page 37)
Two 9" x 12" (22.5 x 30 cm),
   6-mm thick craft foam sheets
   (in different colors)
Puffy paint or glitter glue (recipes at left)
Net or mesh bag, closed at bottom
   (as packaged with produce
   at the grocery store)
1 large bead
1 yard (1 meter) plastic lacing
Craft knife
Ruler

Poolside Dominoes

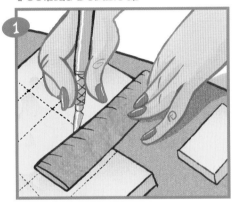

Ask a grownup to cut some different colors of foam into twenty-eight 2½" x 1⅛" (6.5 x 3 cm) rectangular pieces with a craft knife.

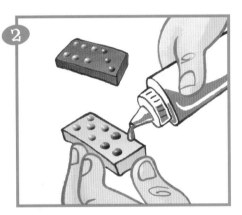

Use the puffy paint or glitter glue to make the dot combinations on each domino (see page 37). Let everything dry overnight.

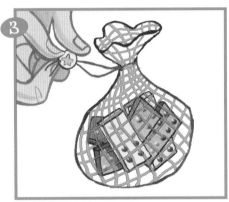

String the net bag with lacing. Slip the bead over both ends, and then knot each separately. Put the dominoes inside, and then cinch the bag closed.

⚠ Watch It!
Have a grownup help with the craft knife.

Paper Potpourri Planters

Recycle old paper to make new fun with these projects for the house—inside and out!

Hearts and stars are just the beginning—you can concoct a whole world of gifts and trinkets with handmade paper pulp!

Get It!

1 cup (250 ml) paper pieces (100% cotton is best), torn to about 1" (2.5 cm) in size

3 cups (750 ml) water

Large mixing bowl

Candy molds or soap molds

Kitchen blender

Hand strainer

White craft glue

Thick, sharp needle or the point of a compass

Ribbon or embroidery thread

Small fabric flower heads

Dried lavender flower petals or cotton balls with scented oil

⚠ Watch It!

Have a grownup help with the sharp needle.

Scented Trinkets

1 Put the paper pieces and water into the blender. Let them sit for 10 minutes. Then pulse (or turn blender on and off) repeatedly until paper dissolves into a fiber pulp.

2 Hold a hand strainer over a bowl, and pour the paper pulp into the strainer. Let most of the moisture drain out into the bowl below before moving to the next step.

3 Place a small amount of the pulp into each mold. Using your fingers, press the pulp down into a thin layer in the mold cups, and then make an indented space in the center of each, just big enough to hold a cotton ball.

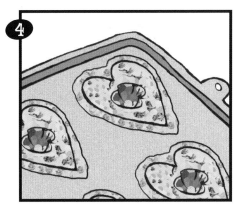

4 Let the pulp flow over the edge of the mold cups at least 1/4" (6 mm) to make a ragged edge around the shape. This edge will hold the shapes together later. Let dry 2–3 days; time will vary depending on the size and thickness of the pulp.

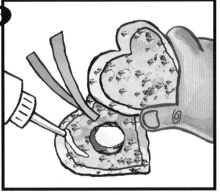

5 Glue a ribbon loop inside the shape at the top; then fill the indent with dried lavender or a cotton ball dotted with scented oil. Glue the halves together and let dry.

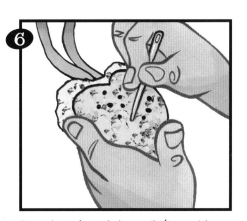

6 Pierce the trinket with the needle (be careful not to pierce yourself!), making random holes to release the scent. Decorate with a fabric flower or bow at the base of the loop.

Get It!

1 cup (250 ml) paper pieces
   (100% cotton is best),
   torn to about 1" (2.5 cm) in size
3 cups (750 ml) water
Large mixing bowl
Candy mold or soap molds
Kitchen blender
Hand strainer
Thick, sharp needle or
   the point of a compass
Ribbon or embroidery thread
Metallic acrylic paint
Medium paintbrush

METALLIC ACRYLIC PAINT

⚠ Watch It!

Have a grownup help
with the sharp needle.

Star Trinkets

Blend the paper pieces and the water in a
blender, and then strain the moisture out of the
pulp according to the directions in steps 1 and 2
on page 25 (Scented Trinkets).

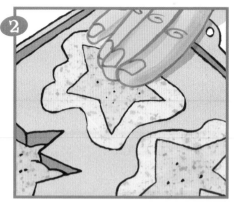

Place the pulp into the molds, filling each completely. Let the pulp edges overlap the mold at
least ¼" (6 mm) to make a ragged edge around
the shape. Let them dry for about 2–3 days.

Poke holes into the ragged edge of the dried
piece with the needle. Then paint the shape with
metallic paint.

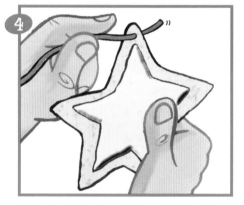

String the trinket through the needle hole with
ribbon or embroidery thread, and hang it as a
decoration or use it as a gift tag.

Get It!

1 cup (250 ml) paper pieces
(100% cotton is best),
torn to about 1" (2.5 cm) in size
3 cups (750 ml) water
Large mixing bowl
Cookie cutters
Kitchen blender
Hand strainer and
flat (paper-making) screen
Thick, sharp needle or
the point of a compass
Ribbon or embroidery thread
Dried flower petals
3 packets wildflower seeds

⚠ Watch It!

Have a grownup help
with the sharp needle.

Flower Surprise Packets

1. Follow step 1 on page 25, but make the pulp using same-colored paper scraps. Add some seeds and petals to the finished pulp before straining.

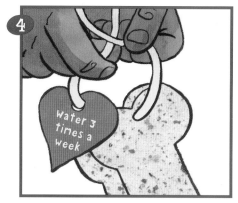

2. Pour the pulp into cookie cutters laid out on a flat screen in the sink. Keep refilling the shapes to the top as the water drains and the paper settles.

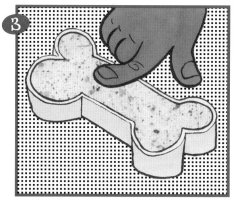

3. When the cookie cutters are full, sprinkle more seeds and flower petals on the wet surface, and tap them into the pulp. Let the pulp drain over the sink for 2–4 days.

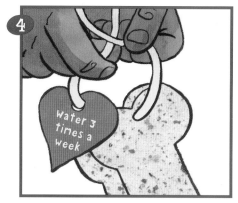

4. When dry, poke a hole through the top of each shape with the needle, and then tie a ribbon through the hole. Write planting directions on a tag, and then use your creation or give it away.

Imagine It!

If you use a food dehydrator, these tags will take only 4–8 hours to dry completely.

5. Plant the packet ½" (1.5 cm) deep in soft soil, and water daily until shoots appear. Then water as instructed on the seed packet.

Stuck-On-You Stationery

Set new trends as you capture the latest catch phrase or the coolest new celeb on your own homemade stickers!

To: _____

Why stop at simple stickers? Make "postage stamps" of your friends by color-copying their photos and gluing them to card stock!

Get It!

Envelope pattern (page 39)

Assorted drawings, photographs, magazine clippings, or decorative papers

2 tablespoons (30 ml) white glue

1 tablespoon (15 ml) white vinegar

Glue pen

Decorative scissors and punches

Regular scissors

Medium paintbrush

Small mixing bowl

Mixing spoon

Sponge

Pencil

Ruler

Imagine It!

If your paper is patterned, attach a solid-colored, self-stick label to create the address portion of the envelope.

Stickers

1 Pour 2 tablespoons (30 ml) of white glue and 1 tablespoon (15 ml) of vinegar together in a bowl, and mix them together with a spoon.

2 Choose some favorite images to make into stickers. Brush a light coat of the glue mixture onto the backs of the images. Let dry for about 2 minutes.

3 Cut (or punch out) your stickers from the dried paper, in whatever shape you choose. To use your stickers, moisten the back of the images and stick!

Envelopes

1 Trace the envelope pattern onto the back of the decorative paper of your choice. Mark the dotted fold lines, and cut along the solid lines.

2 Fold the envelope flaps inward, following the dotted lines you traced. Then crease the folds with your thumbnail.

3 Dab the sides of the bottom flap with the glue pen, and fold it inward to meet the side flaps. Press firmly and let dry.

To-Dye-For Gift Boxes

Don't just play with your food—use it to dye your own unique treasure box!

This box was dyed with blackberries, but try experimenting with other foods to concoct your own cool colors!

Love

GROOVY BABY

Food:	Resulting color:
Beets	pink
Blackberries	purple
Red onions	dull yellow
Radicchio	dull green
Red cabbage	blue
Coffee, tea	brown

Get It!

2-quart (2 L) saucepan
1 quart (1 L) water
Food of choice (see chart page 30)
Kitchen knife (for chopping)
Small mixing bowl
Hand strainer
Small paper craft box
Assorted black-and-white drawings
White butcher paper or wrapping paper
White craft glue
Water-based glue sealer
Scissors
Sponge
Medium paintbrush
Potholder
Rubber gloves

⚠ Watch It!

Ask a grownup for help with chopping and boiling.

Natural Dye

Use the chart on page 30 to choose the color you'd like for the dye. Chop about 1 cup (250 ml) of the corresponding food into small pieces, and bring it to a boil in the water-filled saucepan. Lower the heat and simmer for 20 minutes.

Have a parent help you drain the vegetable mixture. Over the sink, let the liquid dye drip through a hand strainer into a bowl. Pour slowly so that the dye doesn't splash and leave stains! Let the dye cool before using.

Gift Box

Wrap your box in white paper, allowing 1/2" (1.5 cm) extra paper at the top and bottom of the box. Glue the sheet to the box, folding the extra 1/2" (1.5 cm) to the inside. Repeat for the lid.

Next cut and paste drawings to the sides of the box and the lid. You can use any black-and-white art for this step, including pictures from the newspaper, photocopies, or computer printouts.

Wearing rubber gloves, use the sponge to gently wipe color on the paper. Let it dry, and then repeat this step until you have a color you like.

When the dye has dried completely, brush over the box with two coats of sealer, letting it dry between coats.

Follow-It Project Patterns

This is where you'll find a special tear-out section of all the patterns you'll need. If you want to make a pattern bigger or smaller to customize your project, ask a grownup to help you to enlarge or reduce it on a photocopier.

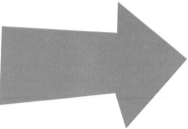

Walter Foster

Walter Foster Publishing, Inc.
23062 La Cadena Drive
Laguna Hills, California 92653
www.walterfoster.com
© 2002 Walter Foster Publishing, Inc.
All rights reserved.

Special thanks to Stephanie Sarracino and the students at Bonita Canyon Elementary School
and to Robyn Allen and the students at Huntington Seacliff Elementary School for their contributions as craft consultants.

Order Code: IT01
ISBN: 1-56010-647-6
UPC: 0-50283-86401-1

Produced by the creative team at Walter Foster Publishing, Inc.:
Sydney Sprague, Associate Publisher
Pauline Foster, Art Director/Designer
Barbara Kimmel, Senior Editor
Samantha Chagollan and Jenna Winterberg, Editors
Carole Thorpe, Production Designer
Toni Gardner, Production Manager
Kathy Beeler, Production Coordinator
Monica Noemi Mijares-DeCuir, Production Artist

Printed in Korea.

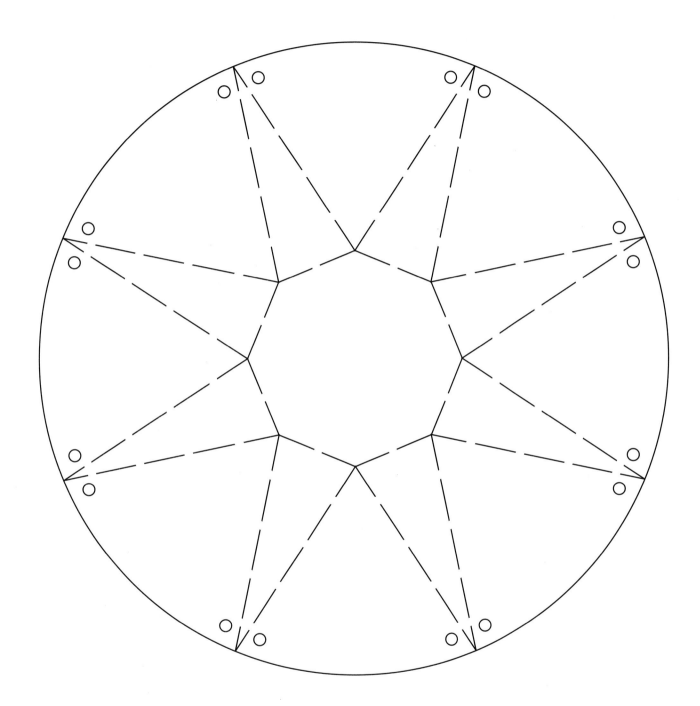

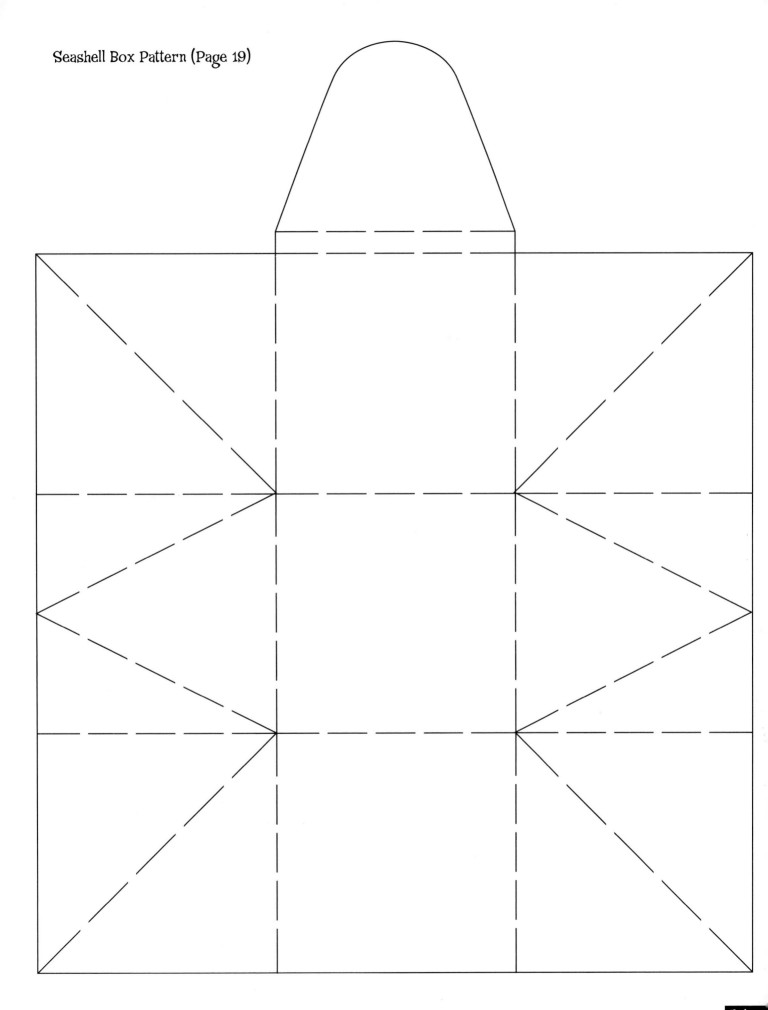

Domino Dot Pattern (Pages 22-23)

You can use the domino pattern as a guideline for the domino dot placement. Or use it as a stencil by punching out the holes, laying the pattern on top of the craft foam, and dotting paint inside the holes. Note: The craft foam dominoes will be a little larger than the pattern.

Envelope Pattern (Pages 28-29)

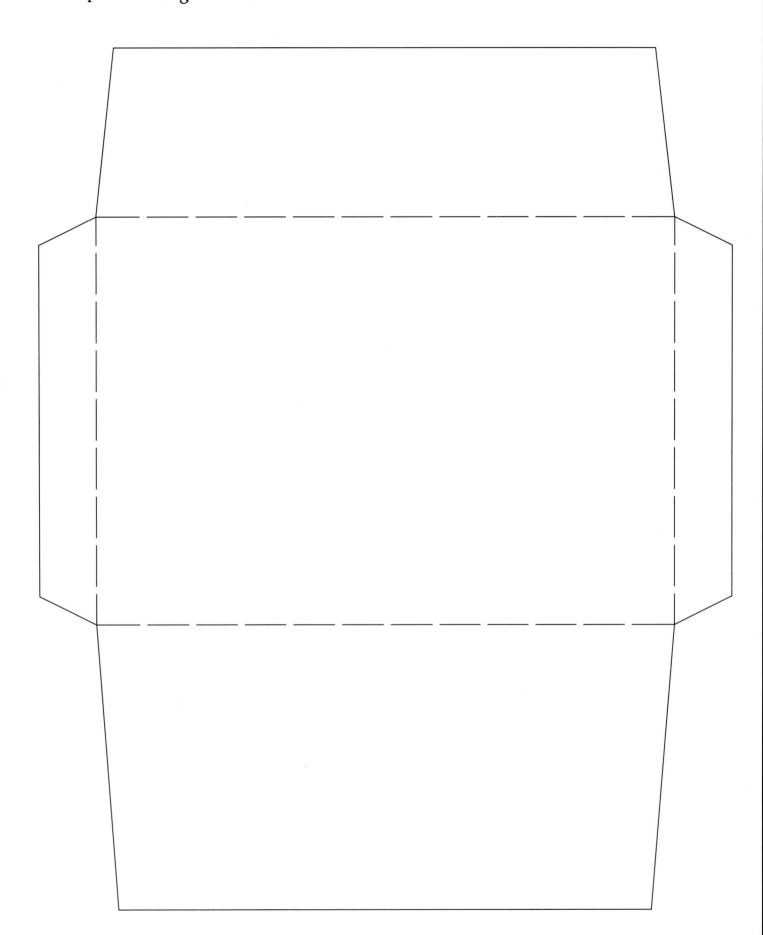